# Double
# Take

*50 uplifting true stories of*
*personal synchronicity*

MICHAEL CLENSHAW

To Liz
with love
Mike
x

THE CLOISTER HOUSE PRESS

First published in the United Kingdom in 2021 by
or The Cloister House Press


ISBN 978-1-913460-35-8

This book is dedicated to my
Grandchildren, currently
Benjamin, Adalyn and Sienna

Salisbury Cathedral painted by John Constable circa 1825

# *Contents*

Coincidence is God's way of remaining anonymous

ALBERT EINSTEIN

# Introduction

Contained within these pages there are 50 experiences spread over 26 chapters that have happened to me during the period of my life. The nature of these experiences can best be described by the word 'Synchronicity' sometimes called 'Serendipity' which is defined as the simultaneous occurrence of events which appear significantly related but have no discernible causal connection.

As the author of these personal 'happenings' I can only say that they vary considerably in the manner of their manifestation. They are not frequent. They are all true. They are all of a personal nature relating to myself. In their own particular way each one has contributed to my own personal belief, either as answers to questions or indications that unseen mechanisms may be at work or in evidence. Perhaps they will help you to remember some of your own experiences that you may have forgotten, and in that way contribute to your own state of experience and belief.

# 1

## *Smoking not permitted!*

For the record, I do not remember any of these events occurring during the first 25 years of my life when I lived in London. My last job before leaving London to settle in West Sussex was spent in a French Bank in the City, where I laboured unenthusiastically for 7 years. It reached a point where I had endured enough and was desperate to 'escape'. So desperate in fact, that in the Spring of 1969 I gave a months notice without having another job to go to.

My parents owned a Canadian bungalow in a sleepy village in West Sussex. I gave up my bedsit in Streatham, worked my notice and drove off into the sunset, aged 26, footloose and fancy-free. Rather irresponsibly one might think!

My first week in this new rural hinterland was spent scouring the local paper for potential 'jobs'. I initially went for an interview at a small factory where they made electric razors. The vacancy was in the accounts department. I cannot remember why but this position did not materialize for some reason. My next interview however, was more fruitful. The position that was offered was at a small dairy that employed about 11 roundsmen delivering milk on a daily basis. My job was to be a 'relief' roundsman covering 3 of these rounds. After my other jobs, this felt like 'heaven' and did not seem like I should be paid for it as I enjoyed it so much! I discovered that I liked being out in the fresh air, being my own boss. Not only did I like meeting the customers, I actually enjoyed meeting people generally, some more than others of course! Also it provided compulsory physical exercise as opposed to my previous sedentary occupation.

It was during this period that my first 'synchronicity' occurred. I had been in the habit of 'smoking' albeit not a lot, neither did I usually 'inhale'. I was more of a 'puffer', not a real smoker at all!

One day one of my customers approached me. He was an elderly gentleman with a deformity of his spine giving him a 'hunchback' look. He asked me if I could sell him a cigarette. I replied that I would gladly give him one.

I walked to my electric milk float to find my cigarette packet. As I looked inside I was slightly dismayed to see that I only had one cigarette left, with no prospect of buying any more before the end of the round, several hours away. I did not mention this as I gave him the cigarette and he thanked me. I was not a regular smoker so did not buy any more immediately. Some days later I must have bought another fresh packet. During the time I was puffing away at these, the same gentleman approached me yet again, with exactly the same request. Once again I walked to the float to access the packet of cigarettes. To my amazement it was the last cigarette – again! I gave him the cigarette, but still didn't tell him it was my last one! I didn't buy any more for a week or two, then I did. The same gentleman was waiting for me this time, leaning on his garden gate. He told me that his wife had gone into town to do some shopping and asked if I could sell him 5 cigarettes. I remember being surprised but once again I walked to the milk float and took the packet out to oblige his request. I could not believe my eyes as there were exactly five cigarettes left. I felt that I had to say something.

"Look," I said. "Each time you've asked me for one cigarette it's been my last one. Now you've asked for five and I've only got five left. What do you make of that?"

"Ah" he said, "The Lord moves in a mysterious way".

I was dumbfounded and gave him the five cigarettes. I didn't buy any more for a very long time, then one morning after a bad night sleeping, I bought a packet on the way to the dairy. I loaded up my float 3 crates high, sat in the drivers seat ready to drive out of the depot. Firstly I took out a cigarette, lit it up, and pressed my foot on the accelerator –

nothing! No power! I had to transfer the entire load to an enclosed motor van, an awkward vehicle to deliver in.

I remembered the significance of the gentleman's previous requests and thereupon decided to give up smoking completely, something I have maintained for the subsequent 50 years.

# 2

## *So you want proof, do you?*

During the time that I worked on the milk rounds I developed a dual interest in antiques, which prompted me to rent half a shop in the historic market town of Petworth in West Sussex. This was a lovely old market town dominated by Petworth House and run by the Leconfield Estate. So my afternoons were often spent sitting in the shop or reading some of the antiquarian books owned by a lady selling them directly opposite me. I came across some books written by a man called Emmanuel Swedenborg. His writings fascinated me as he claimed to have had the ability to visit the spirit realms and return to write about them, and this was over 200 years ago!

I found this quite intriguing and noted that this man had 2 whole pages dedicated to him in the Encyclopaedia Britannica; a reputable source of information before computers came along!

I found the information contained in the Swedenborg volumes so compelling that I was inspired to write off to The Society for Psychical research in London in order to receive their journals. They were situated at No.1 Adam & Eve Mews, Kensington, which is where it was then in the mid seventies. This decision seems to have started a chain of events leading up to my intended visit, which started 3 weeks beforehand. One night, whilst sleeping I was dreaming about something trivial and in the dream something caused me to suddenly wake up. As I opened my eyes in the dark bedroom I saw before me in an illuminated form what appeared to be possibly Arabic writing, which as I looked at it appeared to have clear running water over the top of it. This 'vision' lasted just a matter of seconds before the room became dark again, leaving me very much awake!

About a week later I experienced a similar 'awakening'. This time I saw in my line of vision, English alphabetical letters all jumbled up, in a circular pattern slowly rotating. The letters were white on a black background. Again the vision faded quite quickly. This exact vision happened one more time before the final experience 2 nights prior to going up to London to visit the Society for Psychical Research. I should perhaps mention that this happened during the very hot summer of 1976.

It was a Wednesday night and I was fast asleep. As I was dreaming, I recall that someone pushed me against a wall, which was slightly unpleasant causing me to 'wake up' again. As I opened my eyes, I noticed immediately that there was a feeling in the room of 'static' or some kind of 'atmosphere' is the best way I can describe it. I was by now expecting to see something each time I woke up of course. As I came to, I saw at the foot of my bed slightly to the left, an image of an elderly man's head, side-on, wearing a hat. As I was taking this in, suddenly this 'gentleman' was facing me, without the hat. I was only aware of his 'top half'. I felt myself become afraid, which must have been apparent as I noticed a look of concern appear on his face. I immediately became cognisant that this 'gentleman' was aware of me and my emotions! I looked at him again and he was standing at the foot of my bed. He reached into his left hand jacket pocket and took out a piece of paper. He held it up in front of him and as he started to read from it, to my utter astonishment I heard his voice as if in the centre of my head, similar to the experience when wearing headphones, it was loud, resonant, with a cultured English accent.

He said, "The year 1893 was a very providential year".

He then turned sideways and although I could see that he was still talking, I could hear nothing. As I watched him silently reading from the paper, I thought the words 'I can't see you very clearly' as a sort of test to see if he could register my thoughts. Without looking up he moved his arm nearest to me up and down. 'That's better' I thought, knowing now that he could 'read my mind'. Then he was gone. Afterwards I said aloud to myself 'I don't want to see anything like this again in my lifetime' as it had obviously shaken me. I have since regretted saying this. On the Friday of the same week I travelled to Kensington to join the Society for Psychical Research. When I arrived I was dismayed to find the doors locked. There was a bell that I pressed and a lady's voice came through a speaker. It was the librarian who explained that although they were officially closed, she would let me in briefly to give me some introductory papers as I had travelled all the way up from Sussex.

Earl Balfour 1848–1930

As I stood inside I noticed that there were several paintings of past presidents and one of them looked a bit like the gentleman in my encounter, only younger. I asked who he was and was told that he was Arthur James Balfour, otherwise known as Earl Balfour. When I looked for his name in the literature I noticed that he was the President of the Society in 1893, the year he had spoken of.

I shared this story with a lady who I played squash with. She expressed interest and ordered me a library book on his life that took 3 weeks to arrive. When it did, I opened the cover and inside was a painting of him as an older man, which hangs at Cambridge University. I recognised him immediately as my 'night-time visitor'. His full name was Arthur James Balfour and he was British Prime Minister from 1902 – 1905. He died in 1930.

A week later I randomly picked up another of Swedenborg's books where I read 'When an angel or spirit turns and talks to a man, they can be heard at any distance all the while they are facing him. 'If they turn away, they cannot be heard at all, even though they are close by'. This was my exact experience, and reading the book afterwards gave the event added credence.

# 3

## *Books, who needs them?*

Around that time, whenever a question arose in my mind, sometimes I would be drawn to a particular book, on a bookshelf. Usually I would flick it open at random and just read what was in front of me. Invariably what I read I instinctively knew provided my answer, which seemed quite remarkable at the time. It could be any book, but one day it was the bible itself that answered my question. I had just bought a metal detector and was very keen to unearth something with it, so on this particular day I spent the whole afternoon trudging systematically up and down a local field only to find nothing. When I arrived home feeling somewhat disappointed, I flicked open a small Bible and read a passage which said, 'The Kingdom of Heaven is like treasure hid in a field, which when a man finds it, he goes and sells all that he hath and buys that field.'

Some years later I was wandering around the Exhibition of Mind, Body & Spirit in London. During the time I was looking round, I was collecting leaflets and brochures from various stands till the carrier bag I was using was cutting into my fingers. I happened upon a stand run by Stephanie L. She had produced a book by 'automatic writing' and claimed it could be flicked open at random and provided guidance pertinent to the enquirer. I remarked that years previously I had been in the habit of doing just that with any book.

"Why don't you try it?" she said.

I put my heavy bag down and flicked it open to a passage that read 'If the load you are carrying is too heavy, put it down'. I laughed and told the lady standing next to me. She roared with laughter and as she did so, her own bag split and the contents all fell to the floor!

For some years it was my habit to help run the bric-a-brac stand at a local youth club jumble sale to raise funds. It was held in a small wooden building which quickly became packed with people at opening time looking for bargains.

Just prior to opening the sale at 2pm I discovered a book I would quite like to read entitled 'Sod calm and get angry!' Thinking that it looked interesting I decided to pay for it and put it away in the back room when I would read it later. During the jumble sale, a great throng of people entered the building and there was much bustling and jostling to get near the items on sale. At one point a lady approached our table. She stood out from the crowd in that she was very smartly dressed for this occasion. She wore a smart black dress and coat with a matching hat. She picked up a small metal cap badge made in the insignia of a crown and handed it to me asking,

"Can you tell me what this badge represents?"

I looked at it intently but was no wiser and had to admit that sadly I did not know its meaning or origin. I handed it back to her. At the end of the sale we cleared everything away which usually took some time. I remembered the book I had put aside and went to retrieve it. I could not resist having a sneaky look and was utterly amazed to see that on opening this little book, there was a drawing of the exact same crown on EVERY page!

# 4

## Lightning strikes!

These next four synchronicity stories are perhaps the most dramatic and powerful of all as they involved the use of natural sunlight and also a rare form of lightning.

I was in my 30's, still a milkman, still single and living at home with my mother. My father had passed on a few years earlier, his early death hastened by a lifetime habit of smoking. It was late afternoon. I had finished my milk round that day and was relaxing. It was very dark outside and had come on to rain. There was a ring at the doorbell. It was my Insurance Agent, a lady called Joyce who regularly called about once a month to collect my premium. I had barely opened the front door to her when there was a blinding flash of light from outside accompanied by the most intense explosion that I have had the misfortune to witness. Without another word being said, we all instinctively ran indoors away from the explosion. When we eventually had the courage to go outside there was no evidence of any damage to be seen. It wasn't until the next day that I encountered 2 people who had seen what had happened. They were sitting in a car sheltering from the rain when they saw a 'ball of light' float down from the sky. It landed in an empty field adjacent to our local school about 150 yards from my home. It exploded upon landing. It evidently was an instance of 'ball lightning' a fairly rare phenomenon that has been little documented. You may wonder where the synchronicity is here. That very week I had borrowed a book from our local library on the subject of 'Appearances of the

Virgin Mary' specifically the one at Fatima in 1917 known as 'The Miracle of the Sun'. When I read the book after this event it pointed out that the appearances were often accompanied by instances of 'ball lightning'. I was stunned by the significance of this.

# 5

## *Hello sunbeam!*

This next story involved the use of sunlight, not lightning. I was 40 years of age before I got married. I was not a churchgoer, but my fiancée Gill was a Roman Catholic and we were allowed to be married at The Parish Church of St. Mary the Virgin in Petworth and I have only just now realised the significance of this to the preceding story! The day itself was of brilliant sunshine, a sharp contrast to the previous Saturday when a friend had got married and the heavens had opened that day. After the reception we drove to Salisbury, a special place for us as we had spent a weekend there a short time earlier. The next day, Sunday, we felt it would be appropriate to attend the morning service in Salisbury Cathedral (which I later discovered has the highest spire in

England at 123 metres.) This was formerly known as the Cathedral Church of the Blessed Virgin Mary, another similarity. During the service, bearing in mind that it was the end of October, I became aware of the all-pervading cold emanating from the predominance of natural stone. This feeling caused me to turn to Gill at one point and observe rather drily that,

"I always thought God's house would be warm".

In the space of less than one nanosecond of uttering these words a direct beam of sunlight lit me up.

It was just on me and nowhere else!

The sun had pierced an upper window and beamed down on me at the precise moment of uttering these words.

We were both silently stunned. We later bought an etching of the cathedral to remember our experience and made a note of this 'happening' on the back.

It was 26 years later and we were living in the same bungalow, having brought up two daughters who had now 'flown the nest'. As I approached our front door to see if there was any post I was dismayed to observe what appeared to be 'bits of silver' all over the coconut mat by the front door. Thinking we must have brought something in on our shoes, I called to my wife who could not understand it either. The hall is always dark as there is an overhanging carport outside which effectively stops any light coming in. I opened the front door to get a better look at what this 'mess' was and it immediately disappeared. I felt rather foolish as I realised it was the sun that had caused this illusion. This had never happened before in all the 40 years I had lived here. It was in March 2003 and the morning sun was fairly low and I think it had bounced off the roof of the car that I had then, a Volvo Saloon, something it had never done before, or since. As I closed the door I looked again at the specks of light on the mat. What I then saw, I shall never forget. The random specks of light re-formed to make a perfect feather, complete with spine and quills! I called my wife to come quickly to see it, which she did. I wish I had taken a photo but it did not stay there long enough.

This last 'lightshow' only happened this last year 2020 during the worldwide Coronavirus pandemic. Each day the news briefings were becoming increasingly gloomy with up to 1000 people dying on a daily basis, including healthcare professionals. It was hard not to be affected by the isolation, social distancing measures and loss of social hobbies, and the sense of pervading anxiety throughout society. I was also experiencing trouble committing to sleep at night and had occasionally had some panic attacks. I suppose I was starting to doubt that there could be a 'happy ending' in any way, shape or form. My wife asked me if I would drive 2 miles down the road to collect some bottles of Aloe Vera from a couple who also organised our sequence dance lessons. I met them in their back garden during which time they showed me an outdoor eating area that they had commissioned. It was quite beautiful and featured a square dining table that let down to double as a coffee table also. As I was admiring it I became aware of the outline of a perfect heart formed of light on one of the vertical posts. I remarked on it and we quickly realised that it was formed by a reflection of the sun shining off a place mat, which was on the table.

After a brief chat I was given the 3 bottles of Aloe Vera in a custom made box with the word 'Forever' along the bottom and at each end of this word was the identical heart shape we had seen on the post.

I felt as if I was being told 'Don't ever doubt that you are forever loved'. It was a powerful message that I needed to hear at that time. I had a similar message once before on the same theme 40 years earlier, but we will come to that one at the end of this book.

When I was about 30 as I was driving to work one day I asked God in my head how I would die. Simultaneously a blackbird flew out from the left-hand side and went straight under the car. As I looked in the reversing mirror I noticed it was killed outright. 'That's quick,' I thought.

When I was about 60, also as I was driving along I asked 'when' I might die. Almost immediately the car in front seemed to slow up, prompting me to overtake it. I had no sooner overtaken it when I was forced to stop because of a tractor and trailer up ahead carrying some hay. It's number plate read URV 224 which I was drawn to interpret as 'You arrive in 2024' or in radio parlance 'You rendez-vous in 2024' when I would be 81 years of age. Whether this is correct only others will know. If it is so then it will mean that the end of events is already known years before. Who knows?

# 6

## *You're not on your own!*

This next series of events occurred during a 10 year period that I was undertaking a job for a local charity which involved me working from home and organising volunteer drivers to take vulnerable people from our community to hospital, doctors, dentists etc. I found it initially quite demanding and worrying when I couldn't find a driver, which resulted in me undertaking some of the driving myself. This next happening was most strange and if it had happened to someone else I might not have believed it. I drove a lady and her husband to a private hospital in Bushey, Hertfordshire, which was quite a long way from West Sussex. The wife, a lady called Hazel seemed quite nervous as a passenger and apologised to me as she had felt uneasy travelling in a car since her accident, a year earlier. She was unable to walk properly since and was going to see a leading foot specialist that very day. She had been involved in a head-on crash outside our local Sainsburys. The other driver was a young man who had crossed the centre line while fiddling with his car radio and hit her head-on. I asked her if she remembered anything from the day of the crash. "Yes" she said, "the thing I most remember was looking out of the window and watching my own blood run down the road".

Shocked, I sympathised with her and changed the subject. When I returned home that evening, I was sitting down eating my dinner, which was on a tray on my lap. The TV was on. I started to tell my wife about the lady's experience of her accident and my wife became cross, paused the TV with the remote control and said rather fiercely, "I don't wish to hear about that while I am eating!"

She pressed 'play' on the remote control and a woman on the TV said "I watched my own blood run down the road" the same words I had just used. We were both stunned!

On another occasion I had to collect a lady who was in an electric wheelchair. On the morning of the same day I walked up to our local Post Office just 5 minutes walk away. On the way back I noticed a golf ball in the middle of the road that was not there before. I picked it up and noticed it had the 'Nike' tick mark on it. I placed it in my pocket and thought no more about it. In the afternoon I collected the lady in the wheelchair who suffered with MS. As she drove up into our wheelchair vehicle I was stunned to see that her gearstick handle was a golf ball with identical marking to the one I had picked up earlier! In years of playing golf I never ever found another ball with identical marking. It felt as if the universe was confirming that it knew all about what I was doing!

In my job as Transport Co-ordinator I was getting through lots of pens writing down all the different appointments and one day as I parked in front of my local bank I thought to myself 'I must pop across to the stationers and get some more pens afterwards'. As I entered the bank I noticed that there was a blue 'free' pen on the floor that someone had dropped. I picked it up and told the cashier. She looked at me and said,

"Do you want some pens? We have them coming out of our ears and you can have a whole box if you like".

I was gobsmacked as she handed me a box with 100 pens inside. I couldn't believe my luck and they lasted me for a good six months!

One day I took a lady for a hospital appointment and discovered that she had lived once in Balham, where I was born, in South London. She was reminiscing about the war years and told me that she still remembered the sound of the air raid sirens and the engine notes of the German Bombers as they flew overhead. The sounds were different to the British planes.

"They are two sounds I never wish to hear again," she said.

The same evening I had to go to a rehearsal with a small

entertainment group that I belonged to called 'The Allsorts'. Lena, our leader put on a disk of background sounds that was going to precede our wartime medley. She played the same two sounds that had been described to me earlier that day.

# 7

## *You rang sir?*

When I was organising the community transport service, I was fortunate to have a volunteer each day who took the appointments between 10am and midday. After that time I had a second line installed at home to take any extra calls that were late coming in. One particular morning I had been under a bit of pressure and didn't know how I was going to fulfil all the demands. I felt quite tearful and emotional. There was a ring on my doorbell at the same time. I went to the door. It was a man selling household articles and I asked where he was from.

"Liverpool," he said. "We get dropped off by car and picked up later".

I chose to buy a leather to help him make some money, but the thing about him that impressed me was his gentleness and completely unassuming manner. He just made me feel so calm and 'unthreatened'. Some time later I had another 'low' episode and again there was a ring at my doorbell. It was the same man again! He had the same effect on me as the first time and I never saw him again after that. One wonders when you sometimes hear of angels appearing in human guise. He certainly fitted the bill!

My voluntary drivers consisted of both men and women of various ages and backgrounds. If I wanted someone to take a particular person I usually chose someone who lived fairly near the client. On one particular day I had a strange experience whilst ringing a lady called 'Sue'. As I picked up my phone I noticed there was no 'dial tone'. I had the feeling that the line was somehow 'open' and I said

"Hello".

A female voice said, "Michael?"

I said, "Is that you Sue?"

"Yes," she said, "I have just rung you".

I told her that the phone had not rung at all but I had picked it up to ring her! Don't ever doubt that thoughts travel! This happened once more with a male driver called Ron. He was Indian and his real name was 'Rontu' which the Hindus say means 'Gift of God'.

# 8

## *Sizzling sausages!*

One weekend my wife and I went to Center Parcs in Salisbury with her brother and his fiancée. I should also mention that many years earlier I had practised as a children's entertainer under the name of 'Magic Mike' as a means of earning some extra income and did hundreds of Birthday party shows.

On this particular weekend we had taken our bicycles with us to make getting around easier at the Parc. I had chained them together using a secure combination lock that used a 4 digit number to open. On one occasion we needed the bikes to go and play badminton, but the combination lock refused to open. It appeared completely jammed.

My wife's brother, also called Michael was getting increasingly frustrated, and after trying many different combinations I could see that he was running out of patience. In order to lighten his mood, I rather flippantly said "I know, we could try doing some magic" and rather over-dramatically I called out, "Abracadabra".

Nothing happened which was not exactly a surprise! Then quite spontaneously I reverted back to some of my old 'patter' that I used to use for my shows.

I said, "Ah, I know what's wrong. We didn't use a magic wand".

I turned round and picked up a short stick lying on the ground underneath a pine tree behind us. I then used another magic word that I used in the old days,

"Izzy Wizzy, lets get busy, sizzling sausages!" and I touched the stick against the padlock that my brother-in-law, Michael, was holding in two hands. It appeared to spring apart to our utter astonishment and there was a momentary silence as we tried to take in what had just happened.

That evening Julie, Mike's fiancée cooked our evening meal and it turned out to be sizzling sausages!

# 9

## *I'm looking over a four leaf clover ...*

Four leaf clovers are pretty rare. They do exist but you hardly ever find one, even when you are looking. There is a 14th Century river bridge over the river Arun just a few hundred yards from where I live. In the year preceding my marriage I was standing on this bridge with my future wife, Gill. We were absorbing the peaceful view from this idyllic vantage point and standing in a protected culvert near the centre of the bridge. Suddenly Gill bent down and picked up a clover with four leaves. Unknown to me she had asked God to send her a sign that I was the 'right one' for her! I assume this was a confirmation for the affirmative! We still have that original clover in a silver frame 37 years later!

This leads into another similar discovery many years later, once again with Michael, my wife's brother and Julie again whom he was now married to. The four of us decided to visit a local beauty spot where there was a tranquil lake surrounded by beautiful trees. We went for a walk during which Julie confided to me that life had been rather challenging lately. I listened sympathetically wishing I could help her. After looking at the lake, I spontaneously said,

"Lets go across the road. We might find a four leaf clover".

On the other side of the road is a place where there is a natural waterfall with a powerful sound as the water drops down with some force. As we stood near the waterfall I looked down at the ground and saw the largest four leaf clover I had ever seen! I picked it up and felt I had to give it to Julie. Michael then looked and found a smaller one near to it. Julie has kept this clover also for many years, but my wife was a little cross with me that I hadn't given it to her to replace ours! 2 weeks later I was getting out of my car outside her mothers house and noticed a four leaf clover on the grass by the roadside. Gill was over the moon as it was on our wedding anniversary that I had found it!

One Sunday in 2017 my wife and I offered to take a lady to see her husband who was in hospital. I discovered that she was a local author who had written several books about her village called Storrington in West Sussex. We took her to see him in Bognor Hospital. On the return journey when we arrived at her remote cottage which was situated up a narrow lane. She told me to pull up just before the cottage, as it was difficult to turn round otherwise. As I walked round the vehicle I looked down and saw a massive four leaf clover which I picked up and handed to my wife. As I looked down again there was another, also of equal size, which I handed to Joan, our passenger as a 'Good Luck' keepsake.

Joan had wanted us to take her the following day also, which we were unable to do. However that evening a couple walking past her cottage had chatted to her and then offered to take her, so good fortune was found that day!

# 10

## *Hearts of the departed*

Some years ago I was invited to attend a fund-raising concert in aid of the Teenage Cancer Trust. It was held in a church in Kingston upon Thames. My daughter and her then boyfriend Sam, were performing some musical renditions for the audience. During their performance to the great amusement of the audience, a red heart-shaped helium balloon that had been trapped in the ceiling of the church for the previous 3 weeks, chose this moment to 'descend'. It floated down and hovered just above the heads of the audience. People looked up in amusement to see it, and then quite unexpectedly it rose again and ascended to the ceiling! Someone had lent me their camera and asked me to take some photos for them. I noticed strangely that there was also a small red heart-shape in the viewfinder as a symbol, which I did not understand. During the course of the evening the balloon descended and rose several more times attracting great attention each time it moved.

A while later although I looked for the appearance of this balloon it appeared to have disappeared. It wasn't until the concert was over that I spotted the balloon.

This time it was tied around a young girl's wrist.

I said to her, "Oh, you have the balloon".

"Yes"' she said, "I am a keeper of balloons. I look after them and care for them. Even when they have gone down, I still care for them. I have lots at home".

This statement struck me as such a strange thing for a child to say.

Whilst reflecting on this event afterwards I couldn't help but draw a parallel with the heart and balloons representing the souls of the departed being looked after and cared for in Heaven after they have left this life.

# 11

## *You have been warned!*

One day when I was working at my job as a Security Policeman at an aerodrome I happened to have a casual conversation with an ex-employee who lived quite nearby. His name was Geoff. He was known as 'Big Geoff' as there was another mechanic called 'Little Geoff'.

Anyway 'Big Geoff' for no apparent reason said to me,

"Do you know what happens when a turbo goes on a car?"

"No," I said, "what does happen?"

"The engine revs at top speed and you can't turn it off with the key," he replied.

"How DO you stop it then?" I said rather anxiously.

"You just slam the brakes on hard and stall it," he said.

The very next day his words came chillingly true. I was driving back to the aerodrome to work another day's duty and as I passed the small cottage where 'Big Geoff' lived, the engine note changed slightly which was very unusual. Within half a mile I reached the aerodrome gates and joined the perimeter track that circled the main runway. As I was crossing the runway, the turbo went and the engine screamed at top revs and I immediately braked hard and stalled the engine. The car had to be towed away and the repair cost £1000. Some time later I told Big Geoff how prophetic his words were!

A few years ago there was a national emergency throughout England when a greater part of low-lying land was flooded. It was very unusual and also unprecedented. Just before this happened I was holding my ipod in my hand and it suddenly selected of its own accord a tune by

Eva Cassidy called 'Gods gonna trouble the water'. A short while later I was out one evening playing billiards at an 'away' match when my phone also played another of her songs called 'People get ready'. Was someone trying to warn me again?

# 12

## *So, you want some answers?*

Although I have lived in my bungalow for a very long time, we had never been troubled by mice or rodents at all until on one particular day I was stunned as I entered the loft space and beheld a wee brown mouse deftly scampering across the cluttered space. I told my wife who was not amused! Like a lot of the population, she was spooked out by these little creatures, although they posed no significant threat to her, other than shock and surprise. At her insistence we contacted a local pest control firm who sent along a delightful lady called Debbie who did a quick survey of the area and suggested we put down some 'bait boxes' to rid ourselves of these unwanted visitors. Debbie continued to pay us regular visits, usually once a month for over 3 years. Even after that time, still we were not free of these 'visitors'. We had a renewal contract sent to us the following year, which amounted to nearly £400 for this 'service'. One day I decided that enough was enough and I said out loud to the universe in general,

"I want to know how these mice are getting in!"

2 weeks later, my neighbour, Beryl who had been away visiting her sister, returned. On the day she returned she happened to cut her finger and called me in to assist as she was elderly and only had one leg. It turned out to be necessary to call the NHS helpline and while we were waiting for further assistance we started nattering. I explained that we had been having a 'mouse problem' to which she replied "Oh, I used to have mice in my loft till my gardener told me what to do".

"What was that?" I asked almost too eagerly.

"He told me to fit wired covers to the outside ventilation grills and I haven't had any since," she replied.

I thanked her and subsequently bought 18 covers, which a good friend kindly fitted for me all around the house. It is now some years since they were fitted and no further mice have been sighted. A saving of £400 for each year!

One day I was driving past a local hotel called The Roundabout Hotel that had been closed for some time and I thought to myself 'I wonder who owns that place?' 2 months later I was on a dance break weekend near Torquay. A lady on the next table suggested that we join their group that evening. When I told her where we lived she said, "My best friend lives near there and owns The Roundabout Hotel".

# 13

## *Have you got the right time?*

One day I set my alarm clock for about 8am. As I awoke I noticed that the exact time was actually 8.11am. Simultaneously as I gazed across the room my eyes alighted on a label on an electric fire that also had the number 811 on it. Later that day I happened to look at a Youtube video taken in America of a Medium's reading and it started with her standing outside a house with the numbers 811 on the post behind her. A week later I was staying in our caravan on a campsite and woke up as I had heard the sound of our 'home' doorbell in my head. I looked at the clock by my bedside and the time was 8.11am.

I was sitting at home one evening and noticed that my wristwatch had stopped at 2.34pm that afternoon and I had not noticed until the evening. I told my daughter of this as she was staying with us at the time with her son Benjamin aged 3.

She said, "Oh, our clock at home stopped this morning at Ten to Ten".

As she said it we looked across to our clock on the mantelpiece and the current time was Ten to Ten in the evening. Weird that I should not notice my watch had stopped and then decide to tell her at the precise time hers had stopped earlier!

A week later I visited a local Amateur Dramatic production with my neighbour, Lena. At the end of the performance she asked me the time.

I said, "I don't have a watch," and turned round to see the clock at the back of the hall, which said Ten to Ten.

# 14

## *Miss you Mum and Dad ...*

About 3 years after my mother had died, I experienced a reassurance that we were still connected. I was driving an old camper van past her last residence, a place called White Horse Court. I was in a stream of traffic, which suddenly came to a stop directly level with where she had lived. I looked wistfully up to her old flat, remembering her. Elvis Presley was singing on a tape 'Loving You'. I looked at the car directly in front of me and noticed the registration number was ELV 1S, a rare number plate. The sentiments of the song directly coincided with my feelings at the time and the man singing the song was Elvis Presley, whose name was on the number plate of the car in front of me. The four factors that came together during this synchronicity were location, timing, audio sound and physical representation.

It had been 48 years since my Dad died and one Fathers Day I thought I would 'honour' his memory by placing a large photograph of his old Hairdresser's shop in the garden room off my main bedroom. In front of the photograph I placed his old ARP badge from the 2nd World War and 3 lapel badges of his old angling clubs as he was a very keen fisherman, his only relaxation from a busy life as a barber. At the end of the day I removed the items and went to bed. The next morning as I woke up I looked across to where I had placed the photograph and badges and in their place I can only describe seeing a 'vision' of a tapestry on the wall where the photo had been. On the tapestry were what looked like ancient Egyptian figures, together with antelopes and other animals. As I looked at it amazed, it started to slide down the wall slowly. At a certain point the figures became lifelike and walked across my field of vision from left to right and disappeared, then the animals likewise. I later interpreted this event as showing me that the creatures from the past have gone into a different dimension and are no longer visible. The whole vision only lasted seconds.

# 15

## The French Connection

These next stories all have a French theme. In 2015 my eldest daughter, Jessica was due to fly to France to take up a new teaching job in Monaco. She had booked a flight to Nice where she was going to share a flat with some other girls. Whilst she was in transit my wife and I were at her mother's home in Pagham, West Sussex. I was trying to attempt the Daily Telegraph Cryptic crossword. One clue that I looked at said 'Nice views might be seen through it' (6,6). I realised that the answer was 'French Window'. When my daughter arrived at her destination that evening she sent us an email with a picture of the view from her new room in the house in Nice. Literally 'a Nice view from a French window!'

This next event I have particularly fond memories of, as it was the direct answer to a fathers' anxiety, worried about his daughters welfare. My eldest daughter, Jessica, was in the process of crossing France by rail to attend a wedding. My youngest daughter Katie was shopping locally whilst I was alone waiting for her in her flat near Kingston upon Thames. I had my Ipad on my lap and my mobile phone by my side. At one point my mobile phone rang and as I answered the call, Katie, my youngest daughter said, "Hi Dad". Simultaneously I looked at the Ipad and Jessica, my eldest daughter had typed "Hi Dad" on Facebook Messenger. As I read the words from one daughter, the other daughter said them in my ear!

A friend of ours invited us to try a small restaurant in Aldwick, Bognor that was called 'Chez-Moi' that was run by an English gentleman who was the chef and his wife who was French. I had been there once before for a French conversation class. When I rang to book the reservation I was told that we were the first booking that day and whatever I wanted would not be a problem as he (the chef) could cook me 'anything'.

We duly arrived around midday and sat at a table. There was no one else there. We ordered our meals mine being a chilled soup, (which was delicious) and a vegetarian meal of Potato Gnocci and other vegetables.

When my meal was placed before me I thought 'There's not much food here for a man's main meal'. I made no comment about this to anyone on our table and proceeded to enjoy what little was placed before me. No one commented on my meal or asked me if it was good. We chatted generally and when we had finished we decided to choose a dessert. Just as we were about to order our desserts, the chef came through carrying another vegetarian meal that he had just prepared, warning me that the plate was very hot. He said that he had cooked it especially for me to try, even though I had not asked him to! I was taken aback as I have never had this experience ever before in any restaurant I have been to. The only explanation I can think of for this behaviour is that the chef must have 'picked up' intuitively that I found the first meal 'wanting' and decided to remedy the situation by 'meeting my need' with more food. Another example that we are all connected, and part of a universal consciousness. I later mentioned to the waiter what had happened and he said that he had known the chef do this before on occasion.

# 16

## *We're all connected*

One day I was asked if I could use our wheelchair vehicle to get a man out of his house for an outing. His name was Dennis and he hadn't been out for months. The request came from his helper, a lady called Hari who was from Cyprus originally. Hari told me that she had been a detective and her husband also worked in the Police force. On the day appointed I managed to get Dennis into our vehicle using the electric winch. I asked where he would like to go.

"Fittleworth," he said "to see the house where I was born".

We drove there in about 10 minutes and it was in a lovely serene spot.

"I grew up in South London," I said.

"So did I," said Hari. I replied that I was born in Balham.

"So was I," said Hari "then we lived in Tooting".

I said, "Tooting was where my father's Hairdressing shop was."

Hari then said, "My Grandfather had a barbers shop in Balham." Whereupon I looked at her in total amazement as my own grandfather also had a barbers shop in Balham from 1896.

# 17

## Sorry if I've wasted your time, Doc ...

When I was about 30 years of age I went to our local GP as I had a lump on my left wrist, which was not painful but I thought I ought to get it checked. The doctor looked at it and said,

"Its harmless. It's called a ganglion and it's a fatty growth. I will refer you to the hospital and they will probably cut it out."

Now I have never had to be a surgical patient and I did not like the sound of it being operated on, though I did not say anything at the time. The hospital duly sent me an appointment for a pre-medical check. I duly arrived at Worthing Hospital and when the time for me to go in and see the doctor I was sitting down in front of him and he said,

"OK let's have a look at it."

I rolled up my left sleeve and there it was – gone! I could not believe it.

"It was there yesterday," I said meekly. The doctor was apparently not surprised and told me that ganglions can do that. He told me that in the old days a doctor would hit them with a heavy book and they would reappear somewhere else. I heaved a sigh of relief and retired gracefully!

Some years later I was on the toilet and experienced a slight discomfort when 'peeing'. A day later the same sensation persisted and I rang the doctors but they didn't have any appointments. The next day I was shocked to see blood coming out of my urine. Fearing the worst I made an appointment for the same day. I was told to bring a small sample of urine with me to the appointment. I arrived at the doctors and asked for a specimen bottle but didn't feel like going then so I waited. I was called in to the surgery about 20 minutes later. The doctor asked me for my 'specimen'. I explained that I had not been able to manage it when I came in. He asked me to try again now. As I started to pee I noticed a small stone land in the bottle with the urine. I experienced no pain, nor was there any blood. When I gave the doctor the specimen he exclaimed that it was highly unusual to get a kidney stone in a urine sample and he might keep it on his shelf as a rare example. I have since heard of harrowing stories from people who have had kidney stones and they all describe the pain as 'unbearable'. I consider I was very lucky and am still grateful to this day.

# 18

## *It's not who you think ...*

One day whilst walking near my local chemist I watched a lady crossing my path from right to left who I thought was someone I knew called Barbara H. As I looked closer I realised that I had been mistaken although she bore a remarkable likeness to her. I continued to watch this lady reach her car and then turned to walk into the chemist shop. I was amazed to see the real Barbara H. walking straight towards me and she said, "Hello Michael". It felt as if life was playing a mind game with me.

On another occasion I pulled up in front of a butchers shop and just as I was parking a Range Rover pulled by me leaving. I looked at the driver and thought 'That's Kathy from my drama group.' I went into the butchers and ordered some sausages. A female voice behind me said "Hello Mike."

It was the real Kathy H who had just arrived. The person I had mistaken for her must have been a close double.

There was one more similar experience to this when I spotted what I thought was a German lady I had taken to hospital getting into a car with a male friend. I went around the corner and saw the actual lady herself!

Another strange happening occurred when I was in our local Tesco buying my wife some flowers for Valentine's Day. I happened to notice a lady for whom I had organised lifts to hospital walk past. Almost immediately another lady that I had helped walked past. Then as I was leaving the shop I spoke to another lady that I had helped over the years. When I got home I opened the local paper and there was a group photo of about 20 people and the 3 ladies I had spotted were seated next to each other in the front row of the photo!

# 19

## Many a true word spoken in jest . . .

The next 3 stories revolve around the courtship and marriage of myself, and my future wife.

In 1979 I was asked if I would take a small part in an amateur play. Although I had performed in public as part of a singing group I had never 'acted' before. In fact many years before that I had openly said that I would rather die than go on stage.

My part was as a French naval officer in a play entitled 'My 3 Angels'.

The 'angels' were in fact convicts.

My character name was Lt.Espoir, the French word for 'hope'. I only had 6 lines and came on stage in the very last scene where I was introduced to 'Mademoiselle Dulay,' played by Gill.

As I entered she asked, "Who is this gentleman?" One of the convicts pointed to me and said,

"This, mademoiselle, is the future," and the curtains closed for the end of the play.

We did not see one another for some time but four years later we were in a pantomime of Hansel and Gretel together.

I played a part called 'Willie Schmell' the village idiot. Gill was 'The Bluebird of Happiness' an alternative to the Fairy.

At one point in the panto I entered on stage in a brief 'fig leaf' costume in a rather nervous manner as I approached 'The Bluebird of Happiness'.

My female counterpart said, "Don't worry, she's not going to eat you!" I replied, "It's not eating I'm worried about. She might want to nest!"

By the time the panto was performed we were 'going steady' and this line caused great laughter from those in the audience who knew us.

Within the year we were married!

After rehearsals of the above pantomime, we would sometimes enjoy a mug of hot chocolate together at her cottage. One day we decided to play 'Mastermind', a guessing game where one person would place 4 different coloured pegs in a random

order and they would be screened from the opponent who would attempt to guess the correct layout. At each guess depending on the accuracy of the attempt the other person would mark a score with black pegs if in the right place and white pegs if correct colour, but wrong position. It usually took a dozen guesses to arrive at the correct solution. While Gill my future wife 'set' the puzzle I excused myself to use the bathroom. While I was 'going to the toilet' a thought entered my head that when I returned for my first move I would select no pegs at all for the first guess, something I had never done before. As I walked past the Mastermind board, Gill was careful that I should not see what she had done.

Gill then said "OK I'm ready, you start."

I pointed to the empty spaces and said, "That's it. That's my selection,", thinking it to be a bit of a light-hearted joke.

She suddenly exclaimed, "You are cheating! You saw what I have done!" Stifling my laughter I explained what had happened. She removed the screen and showed me her 4 empty spaces. In hindsight I suppose I must have 'tuned in' to her wavelength and picked up her thought in the next room while my mind was relatively vacant.

# 20

# *The missing decanter*

One day I happened to look in a glass cabinet in my house and spotted a square antique cut glass decanter that I had acquired some 40 years previously when I owned an antique shop. I couldn't sell it as it had a 'chip' on the lip, although the overall quality was superb. As I looked at it I thought to myself 'Why am I keeping this? I shall never use it'. A few days later I was invited into our dance teachers' house to look at a fridge freezer I was considering buying. As they showed me round I spotted a 'tantalus', an antique device for holding 3 glass decanters, although it held only two. I asked if they knew what it was called?

"Yes," the wife replied, "It's a tantalus but we only have two decanters. We have been looking for over 30 years for a third one, but could never find one to match the others."

I then told them that I had one, which I didn't want any more and it was very similar to theirs. At our next dance lesson I brought my decanter and gave it to Sue, our instructor to take home to see if it was a match. The next week she said that it was identical in shape and form to the other two. The only slight difference being that the stopper was slightly smaller.

It was a nice feeling that their needs had been met by something that I had already decided I didn't want any more!

One day my own needs were met in a seemingly amazing way. I had got into my car to drive to my daughters flat just over an hour away. I had driven barely 5 minutes when I realised that I had forgotten to take my nice woolly hat with me. The wind had been bitingly cold and I meant to take it. I tossed up whether to return for it but decided not to bother. As I reached the security gates of her communal flat complex, I opened the driver's door to get out and punch in the gate entry code. Without needing to walk one extra step there was on a low brick wall an identical woollen hat to the one I had forgotten! Someone had obviously dropped it and it had been found and left for the owner to find. I was amazed but didn't have the heart to borrow it!

# 21

## *Money, money, money ...*

In July 2014 I experienced a most poignant and graphic depiction whilst driving from West Sussex to Kingston upon Thames to see a school musical called 'Dazzle' that my daughter, a teacher, was assisting with.

As I drove through Milford there were two schoolboys on the left-hand towpath walking towards the line of traffic. They were both wearing rucksacks and each one was carrying what looked like an executive briefcase. The traffic had slowed to virtually a walking pace and as I observed these two boys I was suddenly amazed and shocked to see them throw the briefcases into the thick undergrowth at the side of the road. It looked most suspicious but I could not stop because of the traffic flow. My brain was working overtime trying to make some sense of what I had just witnessed. When I arrived at the school and took my seat in the audience I had temporarily forgotten this experience until the characters took to the stage. The central 'baddie' character carried a similar suitcase to the ones that the schoolboys had thrown away! His cronies, who were all 'con-men' or crooked property-developers, accompanied him. At one point the 'goodies' took away his precious briefcase and passed it around just out of his reach. The message of the production was that money and greed never triumph over love and teamwork working together. The scene I had witnessed prior to seeing this production could have been written as a publicity stunt, which captured the essential message of the whole production! I have to say, I still wonder who the cases belonged to and what was in them, though I never found out!

# 22

## *The Shack*

Some years ago I bought a best-seller book by a Canadian author called 'The Shack'. It was a work of fiction and the storyline was about a father whose daughter had been abducted and murdered and how he was later reconciled to the events that followed. During the time that I was reading it, I attended a village Fete, which was held annually in a local boys school. It was hugely popular and very well attended. At one point in the afternoon I suddenly noticed an elderly man rushing through the crowd shouting 'she was wearing a red dress!' I asked someone what was going on and was told that he had lost his daughter at the fete and was looking for her. The same evening I continued to read 'The Shack' and the chapter I read next was where the police found the daughter's blood-stained red dress in a shack and were telling the father of their grisly find. The urgency of the man's cries in the afternoon added a spine-chilling poignancy to that chapter!

# 23

## *To be, or not to be...*

At one time it occurred to me that I had never seen a Shakespeare play. At that time I was in the process of selling my late mother's old sewing machine on EBay. I sold it to an Australian girl. She worked as a seamstress at The Globe Theatre in London where Shakespeare's plays are often performed. She asked me if I was prepared to deliver the sewing machine as it was so heavy. I agreed to travel up to London on the train and then take a taxi to 'The Globe'. Whilst I was in the taxi, she texted me on my mobile and asked if I would like to see one of their plays, in which case she would arrange a 'free entry'. After I arrived I delivered the machine and went into the open-air theatre where I was amazed to see that they were performing 'Timon of Athens' which was being performed in German! The translation appeared electronically on screens at the side. At one point a German soldier appeared on stage wielding a machine gun. This was oddly coincidental as only the previous day I had commented to someone about how much the German people had also suffered in the 2nd World War.

# 24

## I'm expecting a baby!

In November 2016 my youngest daughter announced that she thought she could be pregnant with her first child. 2 weeks later I was shopping for Christmas cards with my wife. At one point my wife turned to me standing beside her and asked,

"Why are you looking at that?"

I was holding a card in my hand which read

'Happy Christmas, Grandson'.

I looked at her and said,

"I don't know. I don't remember picking it up."

In July of the following year our first Grandchild was born, a Grandson called Benjamin.

# 25

## *Associated happenings*

One day I was sitting at the computer at home endeavouring to find out if a certain discount card offered discounts at Marks & Spencer, a large retail chain of shops in England. Before I was able to find the answer, my wife badgered me off the computer saying that we had to leave immediately to go shopping in Chichester, a market town near where we lived. I remember feeling slightly peeved and frustrated to be stopped in my tracks before I had found the answer. However, after we got in the car and I had not driven a quarter of mile when my hands-free mobile phone rang. It was the company I was trying to contact on the computer ringing me on another matter. I asked them the question I had wanted to know and they gave me the answer within 5 minutes of leaving my home. The universe had answered my question!

While I was working at my part time job of arranging transport for elderly local residents the question of rail travel up to London from our local station came under scrutiny. Apparently, in order to travel to London and access the Northbound platform it was necessary to negotiate two steep stairways, one down and one up, an impossibility for anyone with an infirmity or an elderly disposition. In the light of this the Rail Company had decided to make an offer of a free taxi ride to the next station down the line where access was much easier, all free of charge. I was asked to find out the criteria for this benefit, by the committee of the charity I worked for. The next day a gentleman rang me to ask if I could arrange a lift to Gatwick, our nearest airport. I replied that I do not normally cover airport runs and asked why he couldn't use the local rail service that provides a fairly quick direct link to Gatwick. He replied that the stairs at our local station were impossible for him to negotiate. I gave him the telephone number of the rail service that was apparently offering to help disabled or infirm passengers. I also asked him to give me feedback about how he managed to get on. He rang back later saying that Network Rail were arranging a taxi completely free of charge on his intended day of travel and accepted his word that he could not manage the stairs at the local station. This answered the question from my committee and it was the first time in 6 years that anyone had wanted to know before.

In these days of computers and tablets and mobile phones it makes it seem that virtually 'anything' is immediately 'knowable'. One day I wanted to know when the dustbins were going to be collected over the Christmas period, so I confidently opened up my ipad and started to fill in the search string for amenity collections. Simultaneously there was a ring at my doorbell. It was our neighbour from across the road. She had brought me a list of all collections over the Christmas period. She had met my need before the electronic wizardry could. I felt that I had been taught a humbling lesson.

Two years ago I took someone to visit a friend in a Nursing home. The friend's Christian name was 'Nova'. I commented that I had never met a 'Nova' before, and was told that it meant 'new'. 4 hours later I attended an audition for a play that was to be staged in a local church and there I met another lady who introduced herself as 'Nova'. Two 'Nova's' within 4 hours!

One day I remarked to one of my daughters that I had not experienced any synchronicities for some time. The same week I happened to drive into Bury, a sleepy Sussex village about 3 miles from where I live. As I was driving along the narrow village street I saw a lady I recognised from my days of doing amateur dramatics in that village. This particular lady had always helped backstage with the wardrobe. I stopped and passed the time of day with her whilst still in my car. It bugged me that I could not remember her name. Afterwards I racked my memory without success, but still could not remember it.

The following day I tried to recall it again, without success. However the next day I needed to post some documents to my cousin about a relative who had died in the First World War. I needed a substantial envelope as I was posting a paperback book as well. I remembered that I had a 'Jiffy' padded envelope in a bag in the broom cupboard. As I took out the envelope I saw that it had been addressed to a Molly S. a lady that had died 6 years earlier at the age of 96 and had also been our neighbour. However, what completely stunned me was that this Molly had written the name that I could not remember on the envelope! It was Ann D. I then remembered that they had been friends. Molly could not have known that her actions when alive would help her neighbour 6 years after her death!

# 26

## *He's lost his marbles, hasn't he?*

This last story occurred when I was relatively young, about 34 years of age. At that time I was drawn to visit a spiritual community in the North of Scotland called 'The Findhorn Foundation' which was based near Inverness. I had previously read a paperback about the community called 'The Magic of Findhorn' and the book chronicled how they had been ultra successful in growing giant vegetables in virtually pure sand through co-operation with the forces of nature. A lady called Eileen Caddy had also published a book called 'God spoke to me' about how she had tuned in to the still small voice within each day and how it had guided her. So I enrolled in what was called 'The Findhorn Experience week'.

One day after a superb vegetarian lunch I happened to take a walk in the surrounding pine forest. As I walked along the sandy path between the high pine trees there was a solitary glass marble lying on the path in front of me. It struck me that it was a rather odd object to find in the forest but as I have always had a lifelong love of marbles going back to childhood, I pocketed it and thought no more about it.

During that week I was given a copy of their in-house magazine called 'One Earth' and when I opened it to read I was stunned to see a 3 page cartoon story called 'It's the marble season'. The essence of the story likened people to marbles and pointed out how we were all different.

In the story God is playing with the marbles and one particular marble rolls behind a chest of drawers. This marble convinces himself that he is forgotten and that nobody loves him and God has not noticed him roll away behind the drawers. Suddenly God scoops him up in his hand and delivers the following message 'Recognise and accept that you are loved. No marble goes apart from me. I will always love you, through your mother, father, friends and everyone else'.

I have kept this book for 40 years and the message has been repeated in different ways several times and is always the same, that we are forever loved.

# In conclusion

Looking back over these past experiences I offer no hypothesis as to how they occurred. The nature and mechanics of synchronicity are covered in other volumes. I can only say that from a personal point of view each individual occurrence has served to strengthen my faith in the unseen workings of our lives and each single synchronicity has been 'purposeful' in answering my needs and questions.

I have noticed that these events seem to occur when I am 'in a state of belief' as it were. Faith is a difficult word to define as it ostensibly denotes a belief in things that are either unseen or unproven. Not at all scientific, the benchmark seemingly required for most matters in this technological age. Personally I believe that 'Science' has a way to go yet before it can realistically quantify the elements that compose a synchronicity.

Perhaps one day we will understand enough to explain the full workings of nature. Perhaps then we will be able to produce by our own devices a single blade of grass. Until then, let us relax with the knowledge that certain processes are still hidden from our gaze.

Thank you for taking the time to read my book. I wish you, the reader, success in your own life and fulfilment of your needs.

# *About the Author*

Taken some years ago in Amberley, West Sussex , Michael Clenshaw is currently retired and still lives locally with his wife, Gillian, an ex-teacher.

Lightning Source UK Ltd.
Milton Keynes UK
UKHW020848260521
384395UK00007B/65